PRAYING
·WITH—
John Wesley

David A. deSilva

DISCIPLESHIP RESOURCES

P.O. BOX 340003 • NASHVILLE, TN 37203-0003
www.discipleshipresources.org

To my sons,
James Adrian, John Austin, and Justin Alexander:
May you grow into the full stature of Christ.

Cover and book design by Nanci H. Lamar
Edited by Debra D. Smith and Heidi L. Hewitt

ISBN 0-88177-317-4

Library of Congress Catalog Card No. 00-102927

DR317

Contents

INTRODUCTION

*I*n 1733 John Wesley compiled "A Collection of Forms of Prayer for Every Day of the Week" for his own use and for others who sought a spiritual discipline by which to grow in virtue, in service, and into the image of Christ. This cycle of prayers captures much that would come to characterize the distinctive contribution of Methodists to the universal church. Here we find the commitment to daily improvement in particular Christian virtues, the exercises in accountability (if only to oneself before God), and the implicit articulation of Wesley's vision for going on toward perfection in love for God and neighbor.

Wesley's forms for daily prayer seek to nurture six virtues that he considered indispensable for Christian discipleship. These are love for God, love for neighbor, humility, mortification, resignation, and gratitude. Morning and evening prayers provide a means for growth in each virtue. The morning devotion introduces the participant to the virtue that is to be the focus for that day. The evening devotion begins with a period of self-examination in which the participant reflects on the extent to which he or she has grown in that virtue during the day. The evening prayer provides an opportunity to ask again for God's help in making the day's virtue one's own. Each of the virtues Wesley selected for special emphasis is one that lies near the heart of Christian spirituality, attested by the recurrence of each virtue across centuries of devotional literature and across all denominational lines.

The goal of this book is to make Wesley's model for daily prayer accessible to Christians seeking to grow toward maturity in their faith and walk. As a devotional tool, it will encourage regular times of prayer and reflection that will cultivate core Christian values. Wesley was a realistic man who understood that Christians were called to serve God in any and every vocation, in the midst of the business of daily life. This model seeks to prepare Christians to use daily activities for spiritual growth and for advancing God's purposes.

How to Use These Exercises

The prayers are arranged in a one-week cycle. Each morning's devotion begins with a brief self-examination designed to prepare one for a God-centered day, followed by a Scripture reading, a short time of spiritual reflection, and a prayer that focuses on the day's virtue. The morning devotional time closes with a period of intercessory prayer on behalf of the church, the world, and those in any kind of need. The evening devotions begin with an extended period of self-examination. You will find general questions to be asked daily and particular questions related to the virtue highlighted that day. These are followed by a reading from Scripture, a brief spiritual reflection, the evening prayer, and the Lord's Prayer. The writing and singing of hymns was a vital part of the early Methodist movement, so I would encourage you to use the hymns suggested to close each evening's prayer. The devotions are designed to be meaningfully completed within half an hour.

Each section begins with an introduction to the virtue to be pursued that day. This introduction attempts to describe the virtue and its biblical foundations. You may use the introduction as a devotional reading at the start of the morning prayer time; or you may choose to read all the introductions before starting the cycle, in order to gain a broad picture of the virtues. I urge you to read the Scripture references given in the introductions to tie the virtues more closely with the nurturing word of God.

The prayers cannot have their intended effect in one cycle. The first time through the cycle, you will be exposed to these virtues, learn about them, wrestle with their meaning and value. Only with repetition will the discipline bear significant fruit. Wesley gave no explicit directions for the use of his model for daily prayer, but the most reasonable assumption is that the model was meant for use indefinitely—until the virtues are perfected and become second nature. I would recommend using them for some extended period of spiritual discipline (for example, during Advent or Lent, which are traditional seasons for pursuing spiritual growth more fervently). However, any cluster of weeks you choose will work well. You will probably use my introductions only during your first time through, at most the second. Thereafter it will be sufficient to use the prayers and other devotional aids without preamble.

Commitment to doing acts of charity has been a distinctive part of Methodist spiritual growth from its very beginnings. Wesley could not imagine a life of prayer that was not also a life of service filled with acts of compassion and justice. The General Rules of The United Methodist Church articulate a value system that extends back to the earliest activities of John and Charles Wesley and the group forming around them. This involved doing no harm, doing good as far as one had power, and attending to all the means of grace (Holy Communion, fasting, prayer, worship, Scripture study, Christian conferencing). Ministering to the needs of people's bodies as well as leading them into discipleship stood at the heart of Wesley's reform movement. Visits to the homeless shelter, the prison, and the orphanage characterized the early Methodist movement. Progress in the virtues held up by Wesley in these prayers will be proportional to one's engagement in these acts of mercy and witness. After one cycle through the prayers, you may be led to replace some evening entertainment with visiting a nursing home or soup kitchen, replace some Saturday morning shopping or fishing excursion with visiting the sick or imprisoned, or develop a mentoring relationship with an adolescent.

If you are anything like me, when you ponder the questions for self-examination and the descriptions of the virtues, you will find the distance between yourself and the ideal rather wide. Please do not let this discourage you. Let it spur you on to progress, and be content that progress toward the goal, not arrival, pleases our patient God.

The Revisions of Wesley's Texts

Wesley exerted himself to provide the "serious Christian," as he put it, with devotional aids that assist in growth toward Christian maturity. He sought to lead the participant into habits of prayer and intercession and to infuse the mind with Scripture by weaving scriptural images into the prayers at every turn. These references are noted at the beginning of each prayer, and you are encouraged to use these Scriptures for personal study and reflection before or after praying the prayer.

It is in the spirit of Wesley, rather than in devotion to the words of Wesley, that this book is undertaken. The prayers in this book are based on the prayers of John Wesley. While the underlying premise of each prayer is directly related to Wesley's prayer for each day, most of the words of the prayer are not direct quotations. In some prayers, I have modernized and condensed Wesley's words; in other places, I have expressed the ideas in the prayers in new words. In all of the prayers, I have tried to remain faithful to Wesley's intent and emphasis.

The original morning and evening prayers all closed with a paragraph of intercessions. Rather than reproduce this paragraph, I close the morning prayers with an invitation to the reader to offer up his or her own petitions, following a list of suggested topics. In this way, this book may also help the user become more comfortable with extemporaneous intercession and may confirm him or her in a regular practice of the same, such as we are enjoined to do throughout the New Testament (Ephesians 6:18-20; 1 Thessalonians 5:16; Philemon 4-6; James 5:13-18).

To complete the transformation of Wesley's prayers into a model for devotions, I have suggested short Scripture readings before morning and evening prayers, provided prompts for reflection and prayer to begin each prayer, and selected a hymn from *The United Methodist Hymnal* (chosen to reinforce as much as possible the day's virtue and echo themes from the evening prayer) to close the evening devotions.

SUNDAY

Love for God

Introduction

*L*ove for God is at the heart of the Torah (the Law). Pious Jews of the first century affirmed this twice daily as they recited the Shema (Deuteronomy 6:4-9). When asked which law was the greatest, Jesus replied with a verse from the Shema: "You shall love the Lord your God with all your heart, and with all your soul, and with all your mind" (Matthew 22:37). Love for God is not a feeling we manufacture. It is awakened in our hearts by glimpses we receive of God's goodness and by a heartfelt recollection of the way God first showed his love for us in calling us into existence, in delivering us through the death of Jesus, and in providing us with what is needed for life and for faith (Romans 5:8; 1 John 4:10). As we seek to grow in love for God, the place to begin and to which to return is recalling the signs of God's love for us.

Love for God is not merely a feeling. Love means showing our loyalty to God in our choices and actions, obeying God's commands, and serving God's desires for his church and his world. Joshua highlights the active dimensions of this love: "Take good care…to love the LORD your God, to walk in all his ways, to keep his commandments, and to hold fast to him, and to serve him with all your heart and with all your soul" (Joshua 22:5). Jesus repeats this understanding of love: "Those who love me will keep my word" (John 14:23). God calls us to love him not only with our lips and in our affections, but also in our deeds—deeds that frequently move us into the second core value: love for neighbor (1 John 4:20-21).

As the first and greatest commandment, love for God becomes the center and focusing lens for our lives. If we cannot do something for the love of God, we are instructed thereby not to do it. Positively, love for God invites us to bring integrity and wholeness to every aspect of our life. The illness of idolatry is a divided heart, being pulled between love of God and love of possessions, recognition, or control over others. Such a heart is self-condemned to be full of stress, stirred up by anxiety over a great many trifles, tempest-tossed in the waves of life. If we take to heart the commandment to pour our whole being and strength into love for God, we are already rewarded in this life with the gift of having a centered soul in the midst of a restless world.

Morning Devotions

Self-Examination

1. Was God my last thought before sleeping and my first thought upon waking?
2. What tasks and encounters will I face today, and how may I prepare myself to bring honor and pleasure to God in them?

Scripture and Reflection

1. Read Deuteronomy 6:4-9.
2. Think about the acts of prayer, worship, and study you will pursue this day, and prepare yourself to engage each act with your whole being, energy, and attention.
3. Sing or read "Holy, Holy, Holy! Lord God Almighty" (*The United Methodist Hymnal*, 64).

Morning Prayer

Scripture References: Deuteronomy 6:4-9; Matthew 22:36-38; 1 John 2:15-17

Thank you, God, for setting this day apart from the concerns of this world. Thank you for the privilege of spending this day in praising you and in remembering your acts of love in creating us, redeeming us by the death of Jesus, and giving us eternal hope by Jesus' resurrection and ascension to your right hand. Let your Holy Spirit guide and help me this day to worship you as you deserve. Let your Spirit keep my thoughts from wandering from you, fan the flames of my love for you, and arouse my desire to worship and obey you.

I know, Lord, that you have commanded me to love you with all my heart and all my strength. This is the level of devotion that you deserve in every way. I am drawn to love you by the virtue and goodness of your own nature. I am drawn to love you even more by the kindness you have shown me: giving me life, ransoming my soul, and leading me to the eternal joys you have prepared for those who serve you. Loving you is the goal for which I was created; therefore, I can have no happiness apart from loving you.

So fill my heart with love for you, that it will become the motive for all the use I make of my mind, my feelings, my senses, my health, my time, my property, and the skills I have received from you. Let me love nothing in this world except as love for you guides me, and so keep me from idolatry. Enable me to be more faithful in love for you during what remains of my life than I have been up to now. Make my resolve firm to love you not merely in words or emotions, but through loyal obedience to your commandments and to your work in the world this day and every day.

Prayers may be offered for
- the hearts and devotion of the worshipers of God throughout the church this day;
- the faithfulness of ministers throughout the church to the teaching of the apostles;
- those in need of God's protection, deliverance, healing, and guidance;
- those limited in their ability to leave home, prisoners, and others who are disconnected from the local church;
- family members, friends, and those with whom we need reconciliation.

Evening Devotions

Self-Examination

General Questions
1. Have I done anything today without considering how it might advance God's purposes, whether in small or large ways?
2. Have I been eager to do what good I could do this day?
3. Have I sought God's purposes in all my interactions with other people today?

Questions Focusing on Love for God
1. How have I sought to use this day to grow in love for God?
2. Have I spent time today reflecting on God's kindness and God's character?

3. How have I sought to make this day holy to God through worship and resting in God's love?
4. How did I spend the time that was not occupied with prayer, reading, and meditation? Did I honor God and promote spiritual refreshment throughout the day's activity?

Scripture and Reflection

1. Read John 14:23-24 and 1 John 5:3.
2. Reflect on the spiritual refreshment you received this day in your worship, study, and meditation.

Evening Prayer

Scripture References: Luke 22:42; Revelation 4–5

I praise you, Lord, for washing me in baptism, teaching me your truth and your ways, preserving me by your gifts and kindness, guiding me by your Spirit, and permitting me and all Christians to worship you and feast at your holy table. Be gracious to all of us and strengthen our hearts against all temptation.

Deliver me from everything that keeps me from loving you fully and completely. Deliver me from the desires, ambitions, and emotions that draw me away from serving you and pleasing you in all parts of my life. Deliver me from being so involved in the necessary affairs of work and home that I lose sight of you standing by my side, or that I seek in the affairs of daily life to please myself or others rather than striving to please you in everything. Keep me sufficiently detached from the busyness of life, that I may see you and know your fellowship throughout the day. Deliver me from being half-hearted in my devotion to you, in my prayers and reading of your Word, and in my service to you. Keep my desire for you and for serving you ever growing, ever burning. Give me a lively, zealous, active, and cheerful spirit, that I might do whatever you command.

Deliver me, Lord, from idolatrous love of created things or beings. Keep me from loving anything of this world except in service to my love for you, and only as far as love for you will allow. Above all, my God, deliver me from an idolatrous love of self. I know that you made me to do your will, not mine, and to love myself, as all other created things, only as it serves love for you.

Let my love for you make my soul steadfast and reliable toward you; let love for you bring wholeness and integrity to all parts of my life. Open me up to taste ever more of your goodness and your love, that my desire will always be for you and that I may give you the cheerful, constant, and wholehearted love, praise, and service that is your due. Make it ever my ambition to give you such constant honor and service as you receive from the angels in heaven.

Conclude with the Lord's Prayer.

You may read or sing "More Love to Thee, O Christ" or "When I Survey the Wondrous Cross" (*The United Methodist Hymnal,* 453 and 298).

MONDAY

Love for Neighbor

Introduction

*I*n explaining which law is the greatest, Jesus joined love for neighbor to love for God (Leviticus 19:18; Matthew 22:37-39). The command to "love your neighbor as yourself" is underscored by James as "the royal law" (James 2:8), and by Paul as "the fulfilling of the law" (Romans 13:8-10). Love is not a matter of words or emotions, but of deeds. Considered negatively, love for the neighbor includes doing no harm to the neighbor (Romans 13:8-10), whether by direct action or by participation in a system that inflicts such harm on others. Considered positively, love means laying down our lives for our fellow Christians and human beings by devoting ourselves to acts of kindness toward those in any kind of need (1 John 3:16-18).

Love for neighbor stands at the core of Wesley's own spiritual revival. The General Rules he developed for the Methodist societies focus on these two aspects of love for neighbor quite directly: "It is therefore expected of all who continue [in these societies] that they should continue to evidence their desire of salvation, First: By doing no harm…; Secondly: By…doing good of every possible sort, and, as far as possible, to all [people]." (From *The Book of Discipline of the United Methodist Church—2000*; ¶ 101, page 48. Copyright © 2000 by The United Methodist Publishing House. Used by permission.) The serious Christian must care for the bodies of the needy with food, shelter, and clothing, and for their souls with the sharing of God's word.

The motivation and model for love of neighbor is God's love for all people. Just as God loves and forgives, so God's servants are to "live in love" (Ephesians 4:31–5:2); because God has set such value on each and every human, God's servants are to do likewise (1 John 4:11). James singles out one particular enemy to love for neighbor—namely, prejudice, whether based on race, regionalism, or economic class (James 2:9). Again, God's example leads us past such barriers, urging us to love as he loves and to cut off from our active expressions of love no one whom God would include in his love.

Love for neighbor includes the love that believers are to show toward one another. By calling Christians to love one another specifically as brothers and sisters, the New Testament writers tap into the standards for natural kin to develop an ethic for the church. Siblings were to set aside all competition and seek to cooperate in all things; they were to preserve harmony and agreement at all costs; they were to share without a second thought as any had need. This is the level of love for neighbor set for the church to embody.

Morning Devotions

Self-Examination
1. Was God my last thought before sleeping and my first thought upon waking?
2. What tasks and encounters will I face today, and how may I prepare myself to bring honor and pleasure to God in them?

Scripture and Reflection
1. Read 1 John 3:16-18 and 4:20-21.
2. Consider the people you will encounter today. How can you bring them encouragement, a word of grace, a needed kindness? Consider people with whom you have a strained relationship. How can you arm yourself to do no harm, and even to show love, to these?

Morning Prayer
Scripture References: Genesis 1:26-27; John 15:12-13; Romans 15:7; Ephesians 4:31–5:2; James 3:5-10; 1 Peter 1:18-19

O God, the giver of all good gifts, thank you for giving me this day in which to renew my commitment to walk in your ways. Help me perceive the ways in which I may improve my obedience this day. Be present at all times, in every task, in whatever company I will keep this day; let your love be my compass throughout today's journey.

You have made all people in your own image, and each person is capable of knowing and loving you. Do not permit me to exclude any person from my loving care, but let me treat each person with that tender love and respect that is due all your children. You have commanded me to show love to others as proof of my love for you. Let no person's words or actions tempt me away from giving you the service you command; rather, let me love for your sake even those who are unkind and hostile to me.

Open my eyes to see the opportunities you will give me to help those in any kind of need. Make me diligent and bold to provide for the hungry and homeless, comfort the disheartened, and protect the oppressed. Grant me the wisdom and courage to teach those who are unmindful of you, strengthen the weak in faith, encourage my sisters and brothers, and warn the wicked, always with gentleness and compassion. Move me to pray for those whom I cannot reach directly with my service.

Let your love for me, blessed Savior, be the pattern for my love for others. You gave your life for my salvation. Let no possession be so important to me that I am not willing to give it up for the everlasting good of my fellow Christians. They are members of your body; therefore, I will cherish them.

Extend your mercy to all people, and let them become your faithful servants. Let all Christians live up to the holy name that they profess. You established the worth of all humans by giving your precious blood for them. Set the value you place on each person I shall meet today firmly before my eyes, and let me love as you have loved.

Prayers may be offered for
- the awakening of the church in every corner to its great calling;
- racial reconciliation and peace with justice throughout the world;
- those in need of God's protection, deliverance, healing, and guidance;
- family members, friends, and those with whom we need to be reconciled.

Evening Devotions

Self-Examination

General Questions

1. Have I done anything today without considering how it might advance God's purposes, whether in small or large ways?
2. Have I been quick and eager to do what good I could do this day?
3. Have I sought God's purposes in all my interactions with other people today?

Questions Focusing on Love for Neighbor

1. How have I sought to use this day to grow in love for my neighbor?
2. Have I allowed myself to feel and share my neighbor's joy or sorrow?
3. Have I responded to my neighbor's weaknesses with understanding rather than with irritation?
4. Have I yielded to my neighbor the right to have the last word in a disagreement?

Scripture and Reflection

1. Read Romans 12:9-21 and Galatians 6:7-10.
2. Confess your failures and sins to God, and receive God's forgiveness and assurance of love.

Evening Prayer

Scripture References: Matthew 5:43-48; 6:14-15; Luke 6:35-36; Romans 12:17-21; 1 Timothy 2:4

Thank you, dear Lord, for your love and care for me evidenced in so many ways. Thank you for pardoning the sins I have committed this day; thank you for the opportunities to show love that were well used this day; thank you also for sins avoided on account of your guidance and restraint. Let it be my single ambition, my God, to honor you in every thought, word, and deed; and make me bold to invite all people around me to honor and love you as well.

Your love toward me is so patient, so tender, even when I provoke you with my disobedience. Give me such an appreciation of your love for me that I may show the same patient and tender love to my neighbor, especially when he or she opposes me. Stir up within me a zeal to do all in my power, whether in prayer or deed, to promote the safety and happiness of my neighbor; make me active to comfort and relieve all those whom you entrust to my care by bringing me into contact with them. Lord, help me to be peaceful rather than argumentative; help me to be quick to forget an injury and be reconciled to my neighbor, mindful of how many times you have forgiven my provocations. After your own example, make me glad to give good in return for evil, and thus share in the triumph of your love. In all my dealings with my fellow human beings, let me reflect your love, your generous spirit, your desire to do good both to the just and to the unjust. You have so valued each person that you sent your Son for each and every one. Implant, therefore, such a compassion in my heart for people that I will eagerly seek out how I may win them to your love.

Take me, my family, my friends, and my enemies into your protection this night. Refresh me with rest, that I may rise ready to serve you.

Conclude with the Lord's Prayer.

You may read or sing "Jesu, Jesu" or "Lord, Whose Love Through Humble Service" (*The United Methodist Hymnal*, 432 and 581).

TUESDAY

Humility

Introduction

J eremy Taylor was an Anglican bishop whose devotional writings pro-
foundly influenced Wesley. In *Rule and Exercises of Holy Living,* Taylor
wrote that humility was the virtue that distinguished Christianity from
worldly wisdom, being taught first not by the ancient moralists but by Jesus.
Jesus' example is the heart of humility. In sharp contrast to a culture in
which people zealously defended their honor and challenged the honor of
others, Jesus voluntarily set aside all worldly honor—indeed, set aside the
honor he had at God's right hand—in order to serve the will of God (Philippians 2:5-11). When reviled, he did not answer with insults (1 Peter 2:21-25).
Rather than seeking to advance his prestige and power, he made himself a
servant to all and spent time with people of low status (Mark 10:45).

Jesus calls his followers to follow him, especially in his humility. He
warned his first disciples that a disciple is not above the teacher, and that the
kind of treatment that would befall Jesus would befall them as well
(Matthew 10:24; John 15:20). Desire for advancing one's status and defend-
ing one's honor in worldly terms is not compatible with the desire to follow
Jesus. Indeed, one must be free from the craving to be somebody in the
world's eyes if one is ever to be somebody in the kingdom of God (Mark
10:35-46; John 5:44). Spiritual leaders throughout history call us to heed
Jesus' words: "Learn from me; for I am gentle and humble in heart, and you
will find rest for your souls" (Matthew 11:29).

Humility is not a denial of one's own worth so much as it is an adequate appreciation of the worth of every other human being. Humility with regard to one's neighbor, therefore, calls us to act toward others with a full awareness of their equal worth. Achieving this attitude, however, requires that we "do nothing from selfish ambition or conceit, but in humility regard others as better than [ourselves]" (Philippians 2:3). We are to yield to others the courtesies we would otherwise demand for ourselves. We are to keep their dignity in view in all disagreements, rather than insist on winning every argument. We are to allow others to have their way in our life together as much as we would wish to have our way. Such attitudes apply, of course, in matters indifferent to our standing before God; humility does not allow others to have their way where that way means sin, injustice, or oppression.

Humility also calls us to know our place in relationship to God. When we realize that, being God's creatures, we owe it to God to pour our full strength and life into God's service; when we realize that we belong to God to use as pleases him, not as pleases us; when we realize that, however much we grow in patience and acceptance toward others, in service to our neighbor, and in witness to God's salvation, "we have done only what we ought to have done" (Luke 17:10) —then we will have a realistic appraisal of our place under God and that humility of heart that brings rest to our souls and an end to all our strivings.

Morning Devotions

Self-Examination
1. Was God my last thought before sleeping and my first thought upon waking?
2. What tasks and encounters will I face today, and how may I prepare myself to bring honor and pleasure to God in them?

Scripture and Reflection
1. Read Philippians 2:3-11.
2. Thank God for all the blessings given to you. Pray for God's help in all the situations you are facing.

Morning Prayer
Dear Jesus, give me the mind that was in you. Put in my heart that spirit of meekness and humility that you showed as you served the poor and the outcast and as you poured yourself out for others. Keep me this day from seeking the praise and affirmation of people; keep me from longing to

be thought of as somebody in terms of wealth, fame, influence, and all the other empty toys of the world. Make it my whole and single desire to be somebody in your eyes.

Lord, I see the faults and scorn the failures of others quickly enough. Let me have such a keen eye when it comes to my own ignorance, weakness, and sinfulness. Then I will think of myself as I ought to think, rather than focusing on the weaknesses of others. In all my encounters with other people today, let me serve them and serve you in them. Free me from having to have my own way in everything; deliver me from having to win every argument. Place before my eyes the dignity and value of each person I will come across, so that I shall not injure them by haughty words or insensitive actions. Help me to show them respect and love, and treat each one as someone greater than myself. Help me also to be content that other people should think of me as I truly am: weak, ignorant, and sinful. Deliver me from the need to show a veneer of perfection to others.

As you allow me and equip me to grow into the virtues that please you, remind me always that I am only a beginner in discipleship. However far you permit me to progress, and however many opportunities you give me to serve you, I am still making a beginning. Use me this day as pleases you, not as pleases me, for I am your servant.

Prayers may be offered for
- the church and its leaders (both clergy and lay);
- the spiritual awakening of our country and the end of violence and hate;
- those in need of God's protection, deliverance, healing, and guidance;
- family members, friends, and those with whom we need to be reconciled.

Evening Devotions

Self-Examination

General Questions
1. Have I done anything today without considering how it might advance God's purposes, whether in small or large ways?
2. Have I been quick and eager to do what good I could do this day?
3. Have I sought God's purposes in all my interactions with other people today?

Questions Focusing on Humility
1. How have I sought to use this day to grow in my humility?
2. Have I sought to put myself entirely at God's disposal this day?

3. Have I done anything today in order to gain human praise or taken pleasure in such praise?
4. Have I entertained fantasies or desires for moving up in the world, or have my desires focused only on how to serve God and others?
5. Have I given myself credit for things God has accomplished through me?
6. Have I admitted when I was in the wrong?
7. Did my treatment of other people today show honor and respect, or haughtiness?
8. Have I refrained from justifying myself where God's honor was not at stake?

Scripture and Reflection

1. Read Romans 15:1-3.
2. Confess the day's sins and shortcomings, receiving God's forgiveness and love.
3. Read Psalm 51:1-17.

Evening Prayer

Scripture References: Isaiah 53:5; Matthew 25:21

Jesus, Lamb of God, enable me to imitate your humility and meekness throughout my whole life, in my every thought, conversation, desire, and act. Preserve me from thinking too much of myself, demanding all that I think I deserve, or expecting that people treat me as if I were the center of their universe. Keep me from seeking to please myself and to increase my fame or power, and let me desire only to advance your honor and your pleasure in the world. Let my ears be closed to human praise and alert only for your word: "Well done."

You, Lord, are the source of every good gift and every good work. If in any way you work through me, teach me to give all credit and praise to you. Let me be as a clear window, allowing your light to pass through me into the world without claiming as my own what belongs only to you.

You were despised and rejected by people. When I am snubbed by a friend, passed over by an employer, ridiculed by my peers, or treated with disrespect by others, remind me of the insults and disrespect you encountered—you who are Lord of all. If it is for your sake that I am slighted, then let me be glad rather than dejected. If it is for some other cause, then let me embrace the slight as an opportunity to heal me of pride and vanity and ask your mercy for those who have slighted me. I am beginning to be a disciple of Christ, just beginning. Keep my heart humble before you.

You have preserved me from all the dangers of this day. Let me pass this night in comfort and peace under the shadow of your wings.

Conclude with the Lord's Prayer.

You may read or sing "All Praise to Thee, for Thou, O King Divine" or "Lord, I Want to Be a Christian" (*The United Methodist Hymnal*, 166 and 402).

WEDNESDAY

Mortification (1)

Introduction

When Wesley talks of *mortification*, he is not talking about shame and humiliation, which is the more common use of the word in today's language. Rather, he is referring to disciplining ourselves by self-denial. The concept of mortification does not sit comfortably with those of us brought up in a culture of gratification and indulgence. The Greek and Roman ethical philosophers understood that a life of virtue was jeopardized at every turn by the passions: our desires for pleasure and aversions to unpleasant sensations, the emotions that often drive us to dishonorable actions or inaction, as well as the cravings both for material and immaterial goods. A major thrust of ethical philosophy was the mastery of these passions that threatened virtue. This could be pursued through abstaining from pleasurable activities, even engaging in unpleasant ones just to strengthen the will against the power of these passions, and seeking what was sufficient for natural needs without being extravagant or indulgent.

Jesus also understood that our slavery to self-indulgence of every kind stood at the root of our spiritual and moral weakness, but he pressed this even deeper than the philosophers did. When Jesus calls us to deny ourselves, take up the cross, and lose our lives for his sake, he shows us that it is our commitment to live for ourselves and our own pleasures that has cut us off from God and the proper service due God. The remedy, therefore, must be to renounce ourselves and renounce our commitment to please ourselves.

It was with a view to the mastery of the passions of self-indulgence that the church took up the practice of fasting, of prayer vigils long into the night, and even of self-imposed discomfort. Such practices were used and commended by Jesus himself (Matthew 4:2; 6:16-17; Luke 6:12). The goal of such exercises was to weaken the tyranny of the body's desires and aversions, to prepare oneself through small deprivations for victory when tempted in more serious ways.

Every denial of a desire that springs from our human nature (whether a desire to express impatience, to seek revenge, to indulge a lustful eye, to eat too much, or to satisfy one's pride through extravagance in clothing or other purchases) is a step toward freedom for unhindered service to God. Wesley gives us two days each week, Wednesday and Friday (the traditional fasting days in the Anglican Church), to grow in this area. He invites us to find ways, both small and great, to put to death our self-will, our responsiveness to our body's cravings, our servitude to "the desire of the flesh, the desire of the eyes, the pride in riches" (1 John 2:16). The goal is that, by self-denial, we will place ourselves ever more at the disposal of God and less at the disposal of the whims and urges of our indulgent natures.

Morning Devotions

Self-Examination
1. Was God my last thought before sleeping and my first thought upon waking?
2. What tasks and encounters will I face today, and how may I prepare myself to bring honor and pleasure to God in them?

Scripture and Reflection
1. Read Colossians 3:1-10.
2. Pray for the guidance of the Holy Spirit throughout the day, and for the Spirit's aid in resisting and disciplining your urges for self-indulgence.

Morning Prayer
Scripture References: Mark 10:45; John 5:30; 6:38; Romans 15:3

Lord Jesus—my way, my truth, and my life—you have said that I can follow you only by denying myself. You have diagnosed my disease; namely, self-love, a self-serving heart, and slavery to my own ambitions, desires, and emotions. This has been my idolatry: to serve myself as my god, to please myself, to do my own will.

Your own example is my cure. Although you made all things for your pleasure, you did not please yourself but made yourself a servant of all. You allowed yourself to be insulted, ridiculed, and nailed to a cross for me. How can I hesitate to renounce myself for you? Let me not presume to set myself above my master, to do not my will but the will of God. I am too much addicted to preserving physical comfort, to indulging myself, to insulating myself from any unpleasantness. Free me from this addiction so that I can serve you with my whole being, and not merely give you what is left over after I have served my ease and excess. Give me the grace to walk in your steps and to take up my cross daily.

Help me this day to set aside any pleasure or desire that does not have you as its ultimate goal. Let me abstain from any pleasure that will not prepare me better to take pleasure in you. Keep me from being distracted by the pleasures that the world entices me to pursue, which would only entangle me and keep me from drawing closer to you. Cause me to be aware of where my senses, appetites, and emotions would carry me, and let me resist every movement that will not honor you or advance your good in this world. Let me have a small victory over these impulses today, that I may hope for a greater victory tomorrow. Strengthen me to practice fasting, prayer vigils, and other spiritual disciplines. Let me accustom myself to small deprivations, so that no deprivation will ever cause me to be disloyal or disobedient to you.

Prayers may be offered for
- the conversion of the self-centered and of those who live by violence;
- God's leading of this nation and its leaders into the paths of justice and peace;
- those in need of God's protection, deliverance, healing, and guidance;
- family members, friends, and those with whom we need to be reconciled.

Evening Devotions

Self-Examination

General Questions
1. Have I done anything today without considering how it might advance God's purposes, whether in small or large ways?
2. Have I been quick and eager to do what good I could do this day?
3. Have I sought God's purposes in all my interactions with other people today?

29

Questions Focusing on Mortification

1. How have I sought to use this day to master the passions and ambitions of my human nature?
2. Have I done anything today simply for selfish pleasure?
3. Have I made up excuses to avoid opportunities for self-denial?
4. Have I been moved to some unholy thought, word, or act today by my desires or emotions?
5. Have I not only refused to indulge what my passions urged me to do, but done the contrary as a means of self-denial?
6. Have I embraced unavoidable inconveniences as opportunities provided by God for self-discipline?
7. Have I insisted on having my own way in insignificant matters?

Scripture and Reflection

1. Read Galatians 5:13-25.
2. Contemplate the love of Jesus shown at Calvary. Renounce whatever in your life hinders you from returning God's love in full measure.

Evening Prayer

Scripture References: Psalm 16:11; 1 Corinthians 6:19-20; Philippians 3:10-11

My Lord and God, I know that I cannot share in your resurrection without also sharing in your death. Strengthen me to take up my cross and deny myself daily, that I may crucify the drives within me that lure me away from loving you and loving my neighbor as I ought. Silence the voices within me calling me to self-indulgence, to self-service, and to self-advancement, and let me hear only the voice of your Spirit leading me into the ways of love, peace, and obedience.

Let me be dead to sin. Having died with you on the cross, help me not to indulge any sinful fantasies, not to utter words that do not serve your holy ends, not to do acts of which I shall only be ashamed later. Let me be dead to the world. I am told on every side to indulge some pleasure, to acquire some unnecessary toy, to feed my pride by improving my public image. With your help and guidance, Lord, these voices shall not be my master, but I will live in simplicity, free from all worldly encumbrances. Let me be dead to pleasure, when that pleasure does not draw me closer to the pleasures that are in your presence for eternity. Let me be dead to my own willfulness and alive only to your will in all my relationships and undertakings.

I belong to you, Lord Jesus, for you bought me at the price of your own blood. Help me to live the rest of my life in this body for you, and not for my own desires or pleasures. Make me a new creature who does your will.

You are the Great Shepherd of souls. Bring home into your fold all that have gone astray. Grant that I may remember you as I go to sleep, and that I may think of you when first I wake. Let me rest under the shadow of your wings this night and rise to serve you.

Conclude with the Lord's Prayer.

You may read or sing "Take Time to Be Holy" or "Nothing Between" (*The United Methodist Hymnal*, 395 and 373).

THURSDAY

Resignation and Meekness

Introduction

P aul writes that Jesus "died for all, so that those who live might live no longer for themselves, but for him who died and was raised for them" (2 Corinthians 5:15). This is the heart of the virtue of resignation, living to serve God rather than oneself, seeking what pleases God rather than what pleases self. Self-direction is a powerful hindrance to effective discipleship. No person can serve two masters, and those who aspire to know God deeply and serve God entirely must first renounce their claim to be masters of their own destiny and commit themselves to the one aim of discovering and doing what God requires of them. In whatever context we find ourselves—family, secular employment, ecclesiastical appointment—resignation brings an integrated wholeness to life as we seek to will one thing; namely, what God wills. Resignation also liberates the Christian from anxiety about the results of our endeavors undertaken in God's service, leaving the outcome to God entirely. This virtue provides the remedy for the person who is harassed by stress and anxiety about how his or her projects will develop.

Wesley engenders a high view of divine providence: God's ordering of God's world and its destiny. Such a view of the world can produce inner peace as we enter stressful situations (change of employment, marital therapy, or some daunting endeavor) with greater serenity, trusting that God has ordained an outcome that ultimately will be good. Resignation can thus lead one to a rediscovery of the meaning of the lordship of God. On the other hand, some circumstances do not readily seem to be born of infinite wisdom and goodness. Some, in fact, seem to be the result of a cruel and malicious fate, such as the death of a young child. Wesley does not seek to minimize or trivialize the pain of such experiences; rather, he calls us to wrestle with God in such situations until we either come to a deeper sense of God's love and care or, when God's intent for good remains obscured, rest in the hope of God's ultimate victory over evil (Romans 8:18-25; Revelation 21:1-4).

Meekness or mildness in our relationships with other humans emerges as a part of resignation. In our modern context, where individual rights and assertiveness are primary cultural values, this quality may at first seem suspect. However, our tendency to see other human beings as potential hindrances to the achieving of our objectives undermines the command to love our neighbor as ourself. Wesley would have us regard our encounters with other people—even those who oppose our desires—as encounters chosen and designed for us by God, in God's infinite wisdom and goodness. We are to respond according to God's goodness, rather than the neighbor's contrariness.

Morning Devotions

Self-Examination
1. Was God my last thought before sleeping and my first thought upon waking?
2. What tasks and encounters will I face today, and how can I prepare myself to bring honor and pleasure to God in them?

Scripture and Reflection
1. Read Romans 12:1-2.
2. Thank God for the gifts of life, salvation, and all things for which you are thankful.

Morning Prayer
Scripture References: Psalm 40:8; Matthew 26:39; Mark 14:36; Luke 22:42; Romans 8:28; Hebrews 10:7

Faithful God, all that I am and all that I have belongs to you. Let me be so aware of your goodness, love, and favor toward me that I will desire to return to you all possible love and obedience. You have given me so much, my health, strength, food, clothing, and other comforts and necessities of life. May I always praise your holy name and love you above all your gifts.

Please forgive my desire to be master of my own life. As Jesus came to do your will, so I am determined, with your help, to do what you decide for me; to have no more say about my life, but only to serve your pleasure with all my heart. Let me do your will in my every thought, word, and action.

I believe, all-powerful and wise Lord, that you arrange and direct all things—even the small and the unpleasant things—to the increase of your honor and to the good of those who love you. Please teach me to trust your goodness and accept your choices for me. Even when I cannot understand the choices, keep my heart fixed on you. Let me do in everything what pleases you and then, in full surrender to your wisdom, leave the outcome entirely to you.

Jesus, I give you my body, my soul, my property, my reputation, my friends, my freedom, my life. Use me, and all that is mine, as you consider best. I am not mine, but yours. Claim me as your right, keep me as your dependent, love me as your child. Be near to help me, so that whatever I do or suffer today may bring you honor. Keep me constant in my love for you and for other people. Let me not be distracted today by the world's vanities and obsessions, nor pursue any worldly activity except for your sake and as you direct me.

Prayers may be offered for
- the mission and unity of the church and its seminaries;
- those who face persecution for their commitment to Christ;
- those in need of God's protection, deliverance, healing, and guidance;
- family members, friends, and those with whom we need to be reconciled.

Evening Devotions

Self-Examination

General Questions
1. Have I done anything today without considering how it might advance God's purposes, whether in small or large ways?
2. Have I been quick and eager to do what good I could do this day?
3. Have I sought God's purposes in all my interactions with other people today?

Questions Focusing on Resignation and Meekness
1. How have I sought to use this day to improve in the virtue of resignation and meekness?
2. Have I tried to desire only what God desires?

3. Have I received everything that has happened to me, even what I would not have chosen for myself, with gratitude as the choice of infinite wisdom and goodness?
4. Have I, after doing what God requires me to do, left the outcomes absolutely to God's disposal and discretion?
5. Have I resumed my claim to my body, soul, friends, fame, property, or destiny after giving these things to God? If I have lost any of these as a consequence of obeying God's direction, have I regretted giving them up to God?
6. Have I treated other people with courtesy, honor, and a generous spirit?

Scripture and Reflection

1. Read 1 John 2:15-17.
2. Reflect on those parts of your life or those ambitions with which you are most reluctant to part. Speak to God about them and listen for God's call.

Evening Prayer

Scripture References: Psalm 73:26; 1 Corinthians 6:20

My Lord and my God, you see my heart and know my desires. I regret that I have for so long tried to order my own steps and live my life to please myself. Now I sincerely desire to return to you and to give myself up entirely to you. I want to be yours, and yours only, forever. Accept my offering of myself, and teach me how to make this gift beautiful and complete in your sight. Let me serve not myself but you all the days of my life.

I give you my mind; let me use it entirely to know you, your virtues, your works, and your will. I give you my will; let me seek not what pleases me, but only what pleases and honors you. Let it give me joy both to do your will and to experience whatever you have ordained for me. Let me love what you love, hate what you hate, and do exactly as you would have me do. I give you my body; let me honor you with it and keep it holy, a dwelling suitable for you, O God. I give you all my possessions; let me value them and use them only for you. Let me faithfully give back to you, through giving to the poor and needy, all that you have entrusted to me. I give you myself and my all; govern and order me and all that is mine. I give my reputation to you; may it be used to advance your honor in the world.

When I am tempted to think again like the world and to adapt to the company and customs that surround me, let me say, "I do not belong to myself; I do not serve myself, nor the world, but my God. I will give to God what belongs to God."

Conclude with the Lord's Prayer.

You may read or sing "Take My Life, and Let It Be" or "I Surrender All" (*The United Methodist Hymnal*, 399 and 354).

FRIDAY

Mortification (2)

Introduction

O ur focus today returns to the virtue of mortification. Friday was the second fast day in the Anglican tradition. Because Friday is associated with the death of Jesus, it is the principal of the two fast days. Therefore, it would be appropriate to combine the day's devotion with fasting of some kind, if this is medically possible for you. Abstinence from food is a readily accessible and time-honored method by which to diminish the power of natural urges and bodily desires. The regular practice of fasting (denying the body this necessary and harmless pleasure) makes denying the sinful urges easier, since we become accustomed and more able by habit to resist self-indulgence.

Fasting is best pursued when coupled with added times of prayer and meditation on Scripture. The discipline is a means by which we affirm the priority of our conversation with God as the source of our nourishment, even as Jesus did in the temptation story (Matthew 4:1-4). If you choose to fast during the daylight hours only, you may wish to spend the breakfast and lunch times in extended prayer and meditation, listening for God's word.

As the day associated with the passion of Jesus, Friday is also especially suited to meditation on Jesus' suffering and death. Seek to spend time today remembering vividly the pains Jesus bore, and take to heart the fact that he bore them for you.

In *The Imitation of Christ*, attributed to the thirteenth-century priest Thomas à Kempis, we find: "Jesus hath many lovers of his heavenly kingdom, but few bearers of his cross. He hath many seekers of comfort, but few of tribulation. He findeth many companions of his table, but few of his fasting. All desire to rejoice with him, few are willing to undergo anything for his sake. Many follow Jesus that they may eat of his loaves, but few that they may drink of the cup of his passion" (Book 2, Chapter 11).

"Christ crucified" was for Paul "the power of God and the wisdom of God" (1 Corinthians 1:23-25). God longs to teach us the wisdom of the cross. Paul lamented over the many who "live as enemies of the cross of Christ," whose "god is the belly," whose "glory is in their shame," whose "minds are set on earthly things" (Philippians 3:18-19). Wesley invites us to become friendly toward Christ's cross and to let God imprint in our own hearts its pattern of self-renunciation, of obedience to God to the utmost, of detachment from what the world holds dear.

Morning Devotions

Self-Examination

1. Was God my last thought before sleeping and my first thought upon waking?
2. What tasks and encounters will I face today, and how may I prepare myself to bring honor and pleasure to God in them?

Scripture and Reflection

1. Read Romans 6:1-14 and 8:12-13.
2. Identify the drives, emotions, or worldly yearnings that have repeatedly welled up in you and moved you to act in self-indulgent ways. Lay these before God, and ask for the opportunity and aid to gain mastery over them.

Morning Prayer

Scripture References: Matthew 16:25; Hebrews 12:3

Almighty and everlasting God, in your infinite goodness you have brought me safely through the night. Continue to protect me this day and watch over me with the eyes of mercy. Fill my heart with your Holy Spirit, that I may use this day and every day to your glory.

Jesus, Savior, you cast out seven demons from Mary Magdalene; cast out from me all sinful affections. You raised Lazarus from the dead; raise me from being dead in sin. You came to proclaim freedom to the captives; free me from the power my own habits, attachments, aversions, and passions have over me. You cleansed the lepers, healed the sick, and gave sight to the blind; heal the diseases of my soul. Open my eyes and fix them upon you. Cleanse my heart from everything except the desire to advance your honor and do your work.

Release me from my striving to be somebody in the eyes of the worldly minded, and let me be happy to be thought a nobody if this means obeying and following you faithfully. You were poor, without office, without connections; have mercy on me, for I have sought wealth, station, and well-placed friends. You were hated and slandered for proclaiming God's justice and love; have mercy on me, for I have sought security and respect at the expense of following you. You were sold for an insulting price; give me a share of your patience when others underestimate my worth. You were insulted, mocked, and spat upon; let me have a portion of your endurance when I encounter the hostility of sinners. You were nailed to a cross to redeem even me; let no weakness of my flesh make me fail to show you loyalty and obedience.

Keep ever in my mind and heart the sufferings and humiliation you endured for me, so that I will be bold to follow you. As you emptied yourself for me, let me be completely emptied of myself for your sake, so that I may rejoice to take up my cross daily and follow you.

Prayers may be offered for
- the calling and equipping of ordained and lay ministers;
- the healing of the nations;
- those in need of God's protection, deliverance, healing, and guidance;
- family members, friends, and those with whom we need to be reconciled.

Evening Devotions

Self-Examination

General Questions

1. Have I done anything today without considering how it might advance God's purposes, whether in small or large ways?
2. Have I been quick and eager to do what good I could do this day?
3. Have I sought God's purposes in all my interactions with other people today?

Questions Focusing on Mortification

1. How have I sought to use this day to master the passions and ambitions of my human nature?
2. Have I done anything today simply for pleasure?

3. Have I made up excuses to avoid opportunities for self-denial?
4. Have I been moved to some unholy thought, word, or act today by my desires or emotions?
5. Have I not only refused to indulge what my passions urged me to do, but done the contrary as a means of self-denial?
6. Have I embraced unavoidable inconveniences as opportunities provided by God for self-discipline?
7. In insignificant matters, have I insisted upon having my own way?

Scripture and Reflection
1. Read Matthew 16:24-26.
2. Thank and praise God for his commitment to save you, his patience to forgive you, his work to sanctify you.

Evening Prayer
Scripture References: Galatians 6:14; Hebrews 12:15-17

Lord God, I do not ask you to give me the things of this world: more money, better jobs, fancier things, fame. Give them to whomever you desire, and just give me your mercy. Give me Jesus. Give me the gift of whole-hearted commitment to follow him and do his works in the world. I do not pretend that this is a sacrifice on my part. No, it is all to my advantage. Serving you is the best thing I can do for my own soul's well being. Serving you is the best way I can help those dear to me. Serving you brings rewards that truly endure.

Accept my incomplete repentance, have compassion on my frailty, forgive my wickedness, purge me of my uncleanness, strengthen my weakness. Above all, anchor my unstable heart and fasten my attention and my desire all on you. Let me be no longer tossed back and forth between devotion to you and pursuit of the world's toys and trifles.

As I am crucified to the world and the world to me, grant that I may come alive to the joys of heaven. Permit my heart and mind to awaken more fully to the pleasures of Jesus' company and friendship. Let my soul be filled with the delight that comes from fulfilling the purpose for my being; namely, to honor and serve you in every thought, word, and deed. I die to worldly ambitions not to be lifeless but to be vibrant and vital to discover those desires and ambitions that you long to satisfy in me. Give me the joy of uninterrupted conversation with your Holy Spirit.

Be gracious to all who remember me in their prayers or desire to be remembered in mine. Strengthen the hearts of your servants against temptations. Grant that we may encourage one another to love and serve you.

Conclude with the Lord's Prayer.

You may read or sing "Take Up Thy Cross" or "O For a Heart to Praise My God" (*The United Methodist Hymnal*, 415 and 417).

SATURDAY

Gratitude

Introduction

Gratitude was a central value of the world in which the New Testament was written. Those who received gifts or favors also accepted an obligation to the giver, to make a fair return. The Greek word *charis*, used prominently in the New Testament, means "grace" or "favor," but the same word was used for "gratitude." A visual image captured the ideal for the giving and receiving of favors—the three "Graces," goddesses who danced in a circle, joining their hands. There was one Grace for giving a favor, one for receiving a favor well, and one for returning the favor. As long as the circle remained unbroken, the dance remained graceful; if the circle was broken, something beautiful was marred and disgraced. It was a beautiful act to show favor or give a gift; it was also a noble thing to allow oneself to feel thankful and appreciate fully the favor given; it completed the beauty of the circle to make a generous return. Response was to be according to one's means; even the poorest recipient of favors could show honor and render services with a glad and grateful heart.

This dance of grace applies also to the gifts received from God. Greek and Jew alike knew that, since God gave the gift of life itself, it was impossible to repay the favor. All one could do was render to God all the honor and service one could. This debt is intensified in the Christian gospel. Jesus' death was specifically a death for us, a gift that brought us back to God and restored us to God's family. Although utterly unable to repay the favor, we are called to show our gratitude as fully as possible by our worship, our loyalty, and our service. Paul quite plainly indicates what would make for a suitable response: to "live no longer for [ourselves], but for him who died and was raised for [us]" (2 Corinthians 5:15).

Our society impels us to seek more, making us feel that our lives are empty. Gratitude calls us to take stock of what we have received, making us realize how full our life already is. God showers so many gifts on us, but we are in such haste to acquire more that we miss the enjoyment of what he has given; we do not receive his gifts well. We therefore close out the week with an invitation to allow thankfulness to fill our hearts. Only if we ponder how much we have been given by God will we realize how rich we are and how full God's generosity toward us has been. As we ponder God's favor and kindness toward us, we will also understand the depths and breadth of our indebtedness to God. Gratitude moves us to honor God by wholehearted worship and by telling others about God's goodness and generosity. Gratitude moves us to firm loyalty, standing for Jesus and his desires, whatever the cost to us. Gratitude moves us to service, offering our whole selves and lives to the work of him who lived and died for us.

Morning Devotions

Self-Examination
1. Was God my last thought before sleeping and my first thought upon waking?
2. What tasks and encounters will I face today, and how may I prepare myself to bring honor and pleasure to God in them?

Scripture and Reflection
1. Read Psalm 116:12-19.
2. Reflect on the kindnesses God has shown you during the past week. Thank God for spiritual gifts, progress in virtue and in fellowship with the Holy Spirit, material provisions, blessings in relationships, or whatever blessings you have received from God.

Morning Prayer
Scripture References: Psalm 50:23; 145:10; Hebrews 13:15

Giver of all life and protector of your creatures, accept my morning prayer of praise and thanksgiving. You are praised, Lord, by all your works. The sun, moon, and stars speak of your greatness; the animals of air, sea, and land testify to your wisdom and skill; the forests and flowers reflect your majesty and the intricacies of your beauty. In the midst of the chorus of all creation, I also give thanks and praise to you, my Lord.

Fill my heart with gratitude, Lord, that I may from a full heart pour forth praise worthy of you. Help me to know the value and the variety of your gifts, that I will never forget my debt to you. Let my awareness of your generosity prompt me this day to be generous in witness to you and in services that please you. And let me never love any of your gifts apart from loving you, the Giver.

You have created me and sent me into the world to do your work. Help me to fulfill the purpose of my creation and to honor you as you deserve by giving myself completely over to your service. Let me prosper in every work that will bring glory to your name, good to my neighbor, and wholeness to my own soul. Keep me from all those traps and temptations that continually coax me to offend you. Do not let my engagement with the world this day dilute my awareness of your nearness or make me lukewarm in your service. Rather, keep me mindful that I walk always in your sight and that in this short life I sow an eternal harvest.

Hear my prayers for all of humankind. Guide their feet into the way of peace. O gracious Comforter, behold all that are in affliction; let the sighings of the prisoners, the groans of the sick, the prayers of the oppressed, the desire of the poor and needy come before you.

Prayers may be offered for
- the awakening of all people to give God gratitude, honor, and service;
- those who face persecution for their commitment to Christ;
- those in need of God's protection, deliverance, healing, and guidance;
- family members, friends, and those with whom we need to be reconciled.

Evening Devotions

Self-Examination

General Questions
1. Have I done anything today without considering how it might advance God's purposes, whether in small or large ways?
2. Have I been quick and eager to do what good I could do this day?
3. Have I sought God's purposes in all my interactions with other people today?

Questions Focusing on Gratitude

1. How have I sought to use this day to grow in gratitude toward God?
2. Have I set apart time to thank God for the blessings of the past week?
3. Have I given attention to those blessings, not just listing them but pondering each one so as to have a full appreciation of them?
4. Have I considered each of them as an obligation to greater love and stricter holiness?
5. How have I used this week to live out a grateful response to God?

Scripture and Reflection

1. Read Hebrews 12:28-29 and 13:13-16.
2. Sing or proclaim "Maker, in Whom We Live" (*The United Methodist Hymnal*, 88).

Evening Prayer

Scripture References: Isaiah 6:1-3; Revelation 4:8-11

Great and glorious God, you are wonderful in all your doings toward humanity. Accept my heartfelt thanks and praise for giving me life, for redeeming me when I was still an enemy, for preserving me to this day, for guiding me into your ways by your Holy Spirit, and for all the various kindnesses you have showered upon me. All that I have has come from you, Lord; all that I can give you came from you already. How can I ever love you enough or praise your name sufficiently for these and all your favors? My mind is unable to conceive of the thanks due you, even for this gift of coming into your presence and speaking with you.

I wish I had the flaming heart of the seraphim, that I might burn with love for you as they do! But since I am on the earth, I will praise you as fully as I can. I will join my song with the immortal armies of angels and archangels, who forever sing with shouts of praise: "Holy, holy, holy is the Lord of Hosts! Heaven and earth are full of your glory!" Keep me ever watchful for opportunities to do you service, to bear witness to your great kindness, to show my gratitude with my life and loyalty as well as with my lips.

Continue your favor toward me, and take me into your protection this night. Let your holy angels watch over me to defend me from the attempts of evil people and from the suggestions of evil spirits. Let me rest in peace and not sleep in sin, and grant that I may rise more fit to serve you.

Conclude with the Lord's Prayer.

You may read or sing "Ye Servants of God" or "O Sacred Head, Now Wounded" (*The United Methodist Hymnal*, 181 and 286).